Poetry Of Love

MICHAEL F MORTON

DEDICATION

This book is dedicated to love. To those I have loved, lost, and still love with all my heart.

To My Angels Three,
Michelle, Megan, and Tristan

CONTENTS

ACKNOWLEDGMENTS

I would like to very much thank and acknowledge my friends and family who helped me in putting this book together. Specifically, Angela Houston, Michael Pearson, Kathleen Dockstader, and my daughter Michelle Morton. Their keen eyes helped with editing and structure of my poems. Thank you again, Michael.

1 POETRY OF LOVE

What is it

Is it knowing the secret,
That no one knows,
And not changing your mind,
Even when the world does,

Is it perfect imperfections,
Something that never comes easy,
Facing the truth,
And never letting go,

Is it honesty in agony,
Helping without expectations,
The connection of dreams,
An unexpected truth,

Is it joy in happiness,
Sadness in misery,
Acceptance in rejection,
Incompleteness in absence,

Is it speaking without words,
A promised decision,
A quiet understanding,
Happiness in nothing,

Its blindly seeing,
A willingly completeness,
Everything you want,
In nothing you are looking for,

Is it understanding the unknown,
And still knowing nothing,
Discovering time wasted,
Is time well spent,

Is it always,
In spite of,
Patience in endless obstacles,

Seeking the dark to find the light,

What is it,
It is easy to say,
It is difficult to define,
It is impossible to live without.

I wrote this poem on 31 July 2018. What is it? Can you figure it out? Re-read the title of the book and then read the poem again. Then you will know what it is.

A Little While

If only for a little while,
An Angel I did hold,
I was on top of the world,
She was a dream come true,

If only for a little while,
My heart did sing her song,
Harmony we both did find,
One clear and starry night,

If only for a little while,
We talked, touched, and loved,
I didn't want to let her go,
She was worth every effort to keep,

If only she could see what I see,
A future without limits,
But you can't look forward,
In the back of your heart,

I held an Angel underneath a starry sky,
And gave to her my all,
It was only for a little while,
But she will remain in my heart,
Forever.

I wrote this poem on 19 FEB 2014. The inspiration for this poem came from a lady I was seeing for a short time. She is an amazing woman, though I haven't seen or spoken to her in years. I felt very comfortable with her and wanted so much to be with her every chance I could. It all seemed to be going so well, then little signs started appearing. She was always busy, tired and the communication just began to cease. She is an uptown lady, and I am just a good old southern gentleman. I don't believe your social status or politics should have anything to do with whom you love. Although this has come back to bite me a few times, I truly believe that love is love. I don't believe unconditional love is bound by the restrictions of job, politics or the amount of money you have.

One very important aspect of relationships I've learned is that you must love yourself, before you can give love to someone else. No matter how bad you want it in your life, no matter how wonderful their lives may seem, if they cannot love themselves as they are, they can never give completely to you.

I truly hope she is happy in life, and maybe I cross her mind every once and a while as she does mine. It was only for a little while, but she will remain in my heart forever.

Butterflies

When I think about her,
I get butterflies in my stomach,
She is all I've ever wanted,
There is nothing about her I would ever want to change,

She looks at me,
With a light in her eyes I've never seen before,
I look at her,
And see everything I've been looking for,

I can speak to her without fear,
We can talk about anything,
Or nothing at all,
And I'm still happy just to be with her,

The moments when I miss her,
I re-read her messages in silence,
My heart begins to race,
And I smile like a little school boy,

Every moment when I am away from her,
I grow homesick for her touch,
Her smile alone can make my day,
And I tell all my friends "That's Her",

I love to hold her close just to hear her heart beat,
I stay awake just to watch her sleep,
She is my world,
And worthy of all my being,

When I think about her,
I get butterflies in my stomach,
The only thing I would want to change of her,
Is her last name.

I finished this poem on 15 September 2017. The inspiration for this poem came from hearing a woman on the radio talk about how she still gets butterflies every time she meets her boyfriend for a date. I took that thought and wrote this poem. I put my own thoughts and feelings into this poem, as this what I would love to have in my life again.

Alone

You're an amazing man,
Her last words to me,
As I put down the phone,
With the sadness of goodbye,

Everything we were,
Everything we shared,
Everything we were meant to be,
Still lies deep within my heart,

No words with a broken heart,
Ever come out right,
What I tried to say,
Her heart could not hear,

There's nowhere to run,
No place to go,
Where I don't miss her,
Where I don't feel the pain,

I've tried to hide it,
So no one sees,
But the look in my eyes,
Shows the true meaning of loneliness,

These feelings I am left with,
Something's just missing,
But life goes on,
As love always ends.

I wrote this poem on 6 January 2014. The inspiration for this poem came from someone who was very special. I have written about her many times before. That's how I know she was so very special, because I can still feel for her after all these years.

A Summer Young

In starry silence,
Treasured memories I hold in my heart,
Reminiscences of a Summer long ago,
Memories of a Summer Young,

She was an Angel,
With a heart of gold and Stardust smile,
The source of many misty-eyed sunlight smiles,
The song of Nightingales unto my heart,

We stayed up all night long,
Hungry for life and love,
The slow waves flowing over the sandy shore,
The soft moonlight caressing her eyes,

A top the world our first kiss,
The ocean breeze warm against our skin,
Entwined in true loves embrace,
A love story daring and true,

In every boy's life there is a girl,
A girl he will never forget,
A storm that rages within his heart,
And a summer where it all began,

These are the days I dream about,
Days when I see the stars kiss the moon,
When I smell the ocean,
Days when the summer breezes blow,

When I remember a Summer,
It will always be this one,
The summer when I found my heart,
My Summer Young.

I finished this poem on 15 August 2017. The inspiration for this poem came from a very special time in my life as a young man, when I found my first true love. I was 19 at the time, and stationed at Guantanamo Bay, Cuba as a Marine. Her sister was in the Navy and stationed there as well. The night we met, I fell so hard for her. We spent the next week or so together as much as we could. I don't remember all the time we shared, call it age or the Traumatic Brain Injury (TBI) I got in combat, but I do remember being so madly in love with her. She had to leave Cuba and go back to start college. We kept in touch via letters and phone calls and visited when we could over the next year or so. Although we never ended up together, she made a special impact on my life. A summer I will never forget.

Absence

If absence makes the heart grow fonder,
Then I am helplessly fond of you,

As the tides flow in and out,
I count the sunsets until you return,
I can see your shining star,
On the darkest of nights,

Our intimacy more than physical,
I can feel your heart beat,
Every breath you take,
Is every breath I breath,

I can't help but think of you,
Your smile, your laugh,
Is in everything around me,
Even though you are thousands of miles away,

Together our future has no end,
All challenges we will overcome,
Every moment apart,
Our hearts grow stronger,

Though you are not here by my side,
I hold you inside my heart,
Counting the sunsets till you return,
And with every moment,
My fondness grows stronger.

I wrote this poem on 18 October 2013. The inspiration for this poem is again about a very special lady who was in my life. I know what you're thinking, this guy must be a player, all the poems about these women. But the truth is, since my divorce in 2007, I've only really dated (relationship wise) three women, and no not at the same time. I am very selective who I choose I date and call my lady. I have met some amazing people in my life, but very few have touched my heart. Some of these poems are very personal and inspirational to the lady they were written about. But not all of the poetry is about a person, many are just thoughts and feelings inside that come out in my writing. It has proven to be a great stress relief and solitude for my soul.

Another Brick

So many stones I've been given,
As the wall grows bigger each time,
Each brick made of fear and heartache,
With pain and failures deep ingrained,

I sit atop the tallest tower,
My thoughts obscure and dark,
Brick by brick,
I guard my source,

My laughter gone,
My eyes filled with tears yet to fall,
I will not show you inside,
The only way to survive this reality,

Higher and higher,
Strengthening day by day,
Living in a state of numbness,
Empty,

Another brick in the wall,
To keep the waves from crashing down,
A sanctuary from crippling pain,
With roots that cannot be broken,

I cannot be reached,
Nor can I reach out,
Protected by thick colorless stones of isolation,
Sealed by the tears of sorrow and sadness,

Another brick in the wall,
To protect what's left inside,
A retreat to keep me in,
And everyone out.

I finished this poem on 21 July 2017. The inspiration for this poem came from thinking about love and heartbreak. Over the many years of heartache and disappointment, you tend to build a wall around your heart. Every heartache you receive, you add another brick to the wall. Some bricks are bigger than others, and tears seal the wall ever stronger. The wall is a sanctuary from the pain, and you cannot come inside. The wall keeps you safe within, but it also keeps everyone out.

As You Are

You are the one my soul does love,
All I have is my truth,
I trust in Life,
I trust in You,

I will take you with all that you are,
Complications, secrets, past and dreams,
Without exceptions,
I will take you completely,

I don't wish to be everything to everyone,
Just everything to you,
As you are my everything,
I could not ask for more,

As we grow together,
As we continue to change in life,
One thing will never change,
I will always keep falling in love with you,

I tell the world I Love You,
Each and every day,
As I softly whisper I Love You each morning,
Because you are my world.

I wrote this poem on 15 October 2014. The inspiration for this poem comes from my philosophy about love. You love unconditionally and accept a person as they are. To me, it's just that simple.

Gaze Upon The Moon

In the silence of the night,
I see the stars shine above,
From the window of my heart,
I gaze upon the moon,

I find myself trapped in seclusion,
With vivid dreams of empty illusions,
Broken by the yearning of loneliness,
Hoping someday to be found,

No one knows the depth of love,
Until it leaves you all alone,
You feel the ghosts of their lips,
As hope flies away on the wings of time,

Only the ashes remain,
Of what was once my fire,
So much of me is missing,
Sorrow begins to rust my soul,

Stormy tears fall from my eyes,
As I dwell on memories past,
Searching in the weeping rain,
Searching for the half that makes me whole,

This hole in my heart,
I walk around it every day,
And when the night comes,
I fall in again and again,

Each night I gaze into the heavens,
Praying for my heart to heal,
I try not to cry,
For my tears will hide the moon.

I finished this poem on 12 June 2017. The inspiration for this poem came from sitting on my back deck by the hot tub and gazing up at the moon. I was thinking about someone very special that was no longer in my life, and how we would spend time together just being together. Life is meant to be shared, so find that someone you can gaze upon the moon with.

Baby Blue

Baby blue,
soft I see,
In your eyes,
I long to be,

More beautiful as a rose,
More brilliant than the sun,
You captured my heart,
with your soft loves glow,

Baby blue,
soft I see,
in your eyes
I love to be

I wrote this poem on 11 July 2012. This poem is about "Her", the one I have written about many, many times. She has the most amazing and captive blue eyes.

Mr. Nice Guy

Nice Guys always finish last,
Placing others before themselves,
Sharing their vulnerabilities,
Their gentleness mistaken for weakness,

Challenges,
They are not,
The challenge of the chase,
There is no appeal,

Placed upon a pedestal,
Labeled as desperation,
Unconditional respect,
Branded as cowardly,

She says one thing,
But pursues another,
Attracted by their emotionless charm,
And predatory nature,

Mr. Nice Guy will always be there,
But always in the "Friend Zone",
Hoping she will see,
Hoping for the change that never comes,

Mr. Nice Guy listens,
And will always keep her secrets,
In his true self,
She is treasured,

Nice Guys will always finish last,
For there is no wonder in the chase,
Yeah, he's that guy,
The one who's never an option.

I finished this poem on 12 June 2017. The inspiration for this poem came from me, as I am Mr. Nice Guy. I was raised to be a gentleman, to respect women with respect and dignity. I was taught to treat all women like a lady, and my lady like a Queen. It took me a few years after my divorce before I considered dating again. Divorce is not an easy thing to recover from. I have high standards and will not compromise my values just to be with someone, so finding someone wasn't easy. The ladies I met were lovely and intelligent, and said they were looking to find a gentleman. Unfortunately, they went back to the old boyfriends who were said to be abusive and disrespectful. I don't know how many times I have heard "you are such a nice guy", "such a gentleman", "but"! Relationships take two, so I am at fault as well. But no matter how long it takes, I will not change my heart, I will always be a gentleman.

Behind Her Eyes

Behind Her Eyes,
So much beauty waits to be seen,
All the beauty of her heart,
The place where love truly lives,

The message of her heart,
Is written in her eyes,
Shown in her smile,
And expressed through her tears,

Behind her eyes,
Lie silent prayers that will save you from your fears,
She will see in you,
All that others will not see,

The story in her eyes,
A life full of lullabies and goodbyes,
She shares her heart like an open book,
But only to someone,
Who cares enough to read the pages,

In the reflection of her eyes,
You will see the person you want to be,
You will know her heart,
Without a single word said,

Behind her eyes,
Such a beautiful light,
Her smile radiates from within,
With a love for life never experienced before,

She has learned to look forward,
Never back at the obstacles she's overcome,
For she knows the past will only fade,
If you let the future shine,

Behind her eyes,
She deserves to dream her dream,

For she's not one in a million,
But one within the world.

I wrote this poem on 4 Feb 18. The inspiration for this one came from just a thought I had one day after talking with a friend and seeing the fire in her eyes

The Untold Truth

My smile hides the sadness,
My laugh hides the pain,
Things are not as they seem,
And I am tired of pretending,

I walk in this world all alone,
A lost soul out of place,
With a heavy head,
And empty heart,

I want so badly to catch my breath,
To hold tight to something other than a dream,
To wake and feel alive,
No more silence for companionship,

The darkness clouds my mind,
Wishing I could just see,
The Untold Truth echoes from my heart,
And I try so hard to ignore it,

Maybe they are right,
Maybe I get my hopes up too high,
When everyone around me seems so happy,
And I just want the same,

I am tired of feeling sad and empty,
Tired of dreaming the dream,
Tired of wondering why,
Why not me,

What if there's someone who thinks about you when they can't sleep,
And smiles at the thought of your name,
Someone who would make you their whole world,
And you're just too busy to see them.

I finished this poem on 27 April 2015. The inspiration for this poem came from seeing so many couples together, and I was alone. It made we wonder, why not me. You pretend you're okay, and life is good. But that is a hard mask to wear. So many times, I would get my hopes up, only to be let down again and again. But you cannot give up hope; your one is out there. Just don't be too busy not to see them.

Velvet

Tugging at my existence,
Soft memories of the divine,
Calling me yet again,
To taste the sweet fragrance of her desire,

I am lost in her moment,
My eyes can hear her calling,
Our fever shared in boundless hunger,
As the soft lite candle casts but one shadow,

The gifts she bares subdue me,
Her taste I cannot resist,
She intoxicates the air I breath,
Her caress allures my senses,

I submit to her embrace,
As her velvet touch receives me,
My body comes alive,
As she is the fire of my need,

Entwined in her softness,
Our hearts beat in rhythm,
With every glance, every touch, every taste,
We discover every secret desire,

In her chamber of passion,
Our hunger cannot be defined,
Our encounters cloaked in secrecy,
A secret that only lovers know,

Tugging at my existence,
I ache yet again to embrace her fantasy,
Her velvet touch unleashes my self-control,
In this sweet dream of worthy surrender.

I wrote this poem on 8 August 2016. The inspiration for this poem came from a love long ago. It's not too hard to figure this one out, and always brings a smile to my face.

Cheer Up

Are you "Okay" they asked,
As I stare off into space,
"It's not that bad",
"Cheer up, things could be worse",

I sat there thinking,
Maybe they're right,
Today's sorrow is not my end,
Not with so much encouragement to cheer me up,

"You will find that someone",
"The one who will make you laugh",
"The one who will listen",
"The one who will warm your heart"

"You will find the one who's words touch you'
"Whose arms will hold you",
"Whose eyes will see only you,
"Whose heart will ache to make you smile"

"You will find that someone",
"That can heal your wounds of solitude",
"Help you forget the storms",
"Think of all the beauty still left around you",

"Remember",
"The stature of your spirit is not based on your situation"
"It's the choices you make"
"To face life each and every day",

"Cheer Up" they said, "Things could be worse",
So I cheered up,
And sure enough,
Things got worse.

I finished this poem on 2 June 2017. The inspiration comes from talking with friends about finding love. I was dating someone who I thought could be the one, but it turned out I wasn't the one for her. So my friends said, "cheer up", "things could be worse". They were right, I cheered up and met someone else. I am a gentleman, and I treat women with respect and dignity. Unfortunately, the one who said she wanted a gentleman, really wanted the not so gentleman. So again, my friends said, "cheer up", "things could be worse". So I cheered up, and sure enough, things got worse. But don't let that stop you.

CGM

CGM,
Church Going material,
She's the kind of girl,
You want to put a ring on her finger,
Right from the start,

She's the kind of girl,
That makes you smile in the middle of the day,
She makes you feel like dancing,
Even if you are afraid to dance,

When you are with her,
You can feel your heartbeat in every sunrise,
And you can hear your feelings,
In the melody of birds singing on the wind,

She brings so much more to you in life,
For you feel more when you are with her,
You live more when you're with her,
And you want her to be with you,
Because you want nothing more than to be with her,

She's the kind of girl,
You want to hold her hand forever,
The kind of girl you'll walk the whole earth for,
Because she's already left her footprints on your soul,

She can see beyond your faults,
And help you see your vision of life,
She always shares her smile with the world,
The rest is for your eyes only,

She gives you purpose,
In ways your words cannot express,
And the only thing you will ever want to change in her,
Is her last name,

CGM,

Church Going Material,
She's the kind of girl,
Right from the start you want to marry,
Not because she's one in a million,
Because she's once in a lifetime.

I wrote this poem on 26 July 18. This one is self-explanatory. If she's CGM, don't let her go!

A Heart Unhealed

Vulnerable is my future,
My conscious clouded by the unknown,
Time has not mended,
My heart unhealed,

So many wounds have gone ignored,
Against me they do weigh,
Pierced by many a word,
With each tear a little more dies,

Conflict rages inside of me,
Robbing me of my joy,
Reinforced by the silence,
I chase my peace in haste,

I am anchored to the pain,
My reservoir of hope drained dry,
My strength stolen by pride,
Caressed by the anguished hands of sorrow,

Scarred with regrets,
My ordered life has unfurled,
Like an hour glass for all time,
My essence fades with each grain of sand,

An unhealed heart knows not its own depth,
The Song it sings no more,
Weeping with every heartbeat,
Its lonely glass fills with tears,

With a weary soul,
I try to hold on,
For the emotion that wounds the heart,
Is the only one
that can save a heart unhealed

I wrote this poem on 16 September 15. The inspiration for this poem came from just thinking one day about a broken heart.

The Joy I See

The Joy I See,
A life of new beginnings,
Only from the heart,
Can a river of joy flow like this,

The Joy I see,
The rest of life starting now,
A bliss kept from here to eternity,
Two souls joined for life,

The Joy I see,
The happiness within their eyes,
Full of life and wonder,
Is shared with me in a smile,

The Joy I see,
The beating heart of life,
A connection to everything beautiful,
The infallible sign of the presence of God,

The Joy I see,
The source of their smile,
The expression of love in movement,
The sheer surging of life in a moment,

The Joy I see,
A life nurtured and endeavored to live,
Like walking under a sun filled sky,
Every moment a memory to kept,

Its moments like this,
I am reminded of the gifts we have in life,
That there is hope yet for me,
In the Joy I see.

I finished this poem on 31 July 2017. The inspiration for this poem came from watching a music video of the song "Sugar" by the band Maroon 5. In the video, the band travels around Los Angeles surprising new weds by performing at the wedding reception. The joy you see in the couple's eyes, you can tell they are so happy in love. The joy I see in their eyes is the joy I hope to find in my life one day.

Answer's Always the Same

When you dream with a broken heart
The answer's always the same,
And waking up is the hardest part,
Cause you want so badly for it to change,

Awake, I am walking through my memories,
Reliving all the pain,
Pieces of my broken dreams,
I find them everywhere,

My soul is restless,
My fallen thoughts repeat,
I'm running away in fear,
To find her love again,

Drowning in my sorrow,
I feel faith abandon me,
Confusion clouds my mind,
Gripping me with fear,

How can I let go,
Of all I've ever known.
But reality calls my name,
And the answer is always the same

I don't want to fall asleep,
And dream with a broken heart,
Cause I always wake up alone,
And the answers always the same.

I wrote this poem on 9 January 2014. Think about what it like to dream with a broken heart. We've all had a one, and it never gets easy with time.

Something So Strong

Something So Strong,
It cannot be articulated or explained,
It makes you powerful,
Determined beyond all belief,

The coward says there is no such thing,
As they hid in the shadows of its existence,
Their spirit ever so small,
Because they are too small to believe,

Something so strong,
If you let it come into your life,
It will see the most negative parts of you,
And still never leave,

Something so strong,
It can break down all walls,
Defeat all misery,
And send you soaring above the clouds,

Something so strong,
It enwraps over very nature,
It can endure any circumstance,
And reach across any distance,

Something so strong,
There is no greater inspiration,
It defies the rules of reason,
With the magic to change your world,

Something so strong,
In it nothing is impossible,
It has the power to see all people,
It is the source that touches the soul.

I finished this poem on 29 August 2017. The inspiration for this poem is simple LOVE.

Don't Include Me

She's got that look,
Ya she's got that style,
She's got that sassy little walk,
That always makes me smile,

Ya she's got everything she wants,
Ya she's got everything she needs,
But it don't include me,

She knows where she's goin',
She don't care where she's been,
She got all the guys chasin'
But she just calls them friend,

I tried catchn' her attention,
I tried playin' her game,
I tried to show her I was different,
But to her we're all the same,

Ya she's got everything she wants,
Ya she's got everything she needs,
But it don't include me,

So hold on Ol'e boy,
dont go beatn' your chest,
Shes a pistol packin momma,
And you'll end up like the rest,

Ya she's got everything she wants,
Ya she's got everything she needs,
But it don't include me,

I wrote this poem on 18 January 2018. I wrote this poem one night when I couldn't sleep. The words kept running through my mind, so I got up and wrote the basics down in about 5 minutes. The next morning when I was looking at what I had written, I thought it could also be a song. I shared this with some friends, and we all agreed it could be a good country song. So I wrote this with the intent of it being a song, but I will leave it to you, Song or Poem?

Speaking In Love

How does true love speak,
In the embrace where sadness melts,
In the joy of a kiss,
From the lips of a tender heart,

Deep within the fire,
That flows through tender veins,
In the shyness of hands,
That thrill and tremble with a touch,

Love makes no demands,
As love is always spoken freely,
In the search to find one's meaning,
Love is at the heart of our existence,

Loves languages do not erase the past,
But make the future possible,
Love is a choice,
A choice only you can make,

When love is spoken true,
Mountains can be moved,
The roughest seas can be crossed,
And the greatest hardships endured,

When speaking in love,
We speak that of our own,
When speaking in the love of another,
Love expressed in theirs can mean the world,

We all blossom,
When speaking in the languages of love,
It's when we are spoken to in our own,
That we speak with true love.

I finished this poem on 18 May 2015. The inspiration for this poem came from talking with a friend about the languages of love. The topic comes from a book 5 Love Languages. We all communicate differently and learning to speaking in your partner's language will express your love in a way they understand and appreciate.

Edge of a Tear

On the edge of a tear,
I hang on tight,
I don't want to let go,
Emotions I try to fight,

The sadness of being alone,
When she said goodbye,
I didn't see it coming,
I don't know why,

Everything seemed so right,
Each day was bright and new,
I thought I had found her,
I thought it could be a love so true,

But that was just a dream,
To have someone to hold,
To keep me safe and warm,
And never leave me cold,

There's nothing left I can say,
So I'll just sit right here,
And watch the sun go down,
On the edge of a tear.

I wrote this on 6 Feb 14. Just another thought that entered my mind and I wrote about it.

Treasure

The One you should treasure,
But she is not your possession,
She should be loved,
And never a heavy hand upon her,

She is yours to treasure,
Her value greater than all the worlds gold,
Be proud to have her on your arm,
And show the world she is yours,

She should always be built up,
And never torn down,
By the words you speak,
Or the silence you impose,

She should be embraced every day,
With the warmth of your loving arms,
Never pushed away,
Even when your day was long,

Words spoken in anger,
Will hurt her fragile heart,
Never a target of your frustration,
She deserves so much more,

She should be admired for her love,
And looked upon as a gift from above,
Appreciate her commitment to you,
And return her commitment with your own,

Simply lover her every moment of everyday,
With all that you possibly can,
Treat her as your greatest treasure,
And lover her each day as if it were your last.

I finished this poem on 4 May 2015. The inspiration for this poem is simple. You should treasure your woman above everything in life but the Father. For she is a gift from the Father, and the greatest treasure you will ever have.

First Last Time

A part of me is missing,
The part of me I relied on,
To keep me going strong,
That part of you,

Always on my mind,
Memories engraved in my heart,
Visions of you everywhere,
Only make it worse,

When it's the first time,
Your heart says goodbye,
When it's the last time,
You kiss her lips,

I try to forget,
And ask myself why,
When I face the dark,
To see the light,

I look ahead,
But can't move forward,
I dream of before,
And know I can't stay,

So much I could have said,
So much you didn't,
Did we say all we needed to say,
Did we try all we should have tried,

My hearts ever calling to you,
But you never answer,
Stuck in a dream undecided,
Like a story with no end.

I wrote this on 16 May 13. The inspiration for this poem came from talking with a friend about their relationship that just ended. As we talked, I couldn't help but think of my own heart breaks. When it was the first time you had to say goodbye to the one you love. When it's the last time you kissed her lips. Think about how such a memory will haunt you. I can still remember. Can you?

Over Again

I want to go back in time,
And love you all over again,
Back to our first embrace,
And taste our first kiss,

Heart to heart,
Soul to soul,
Over and over again,
I fall for you,

There are moments,
When it's like I see you for the very first time,
And the times we are apart,
My heart grows fonder,

Because every time I look at you,
I am right back where I began,
Falling your love,
All over again,

All that was,
And all that will ever be,
You are my one,
My one and only one,

I love you more than you'll ever know,
You are the inspiration in my life,
The smile within my soul,
The love that gives me faith to believe,

In your love my heart has found its home,
In your arms I find my comfort,
In your smile I find my peace,
You are my today, my tomorrow, and my forever,
Over and over again.

I finished this poem on 4 May 2015. The inspiration for this poem is another simple one, Love. This is how I believe love should be.

Like I Loved You

You are my fire,
That burns within my soul,
You brighten my world,
With the warmth of your love,

When I look into your eyes,
I don't just see you,
I see my tomorrow,
I see the rest of my life,

I hold you in my heart,
Where all my love does live,
I hold you within my soul,
And there you will be till the end of time,

Every moment we are together,
Another dream comes true,
All the stars in the universe,
Cannot replace the light you bring into my life,

I love you for who you are,
And who I am when I am with you,
You are the very reason,
There is hope within my life,

You have my love,
You have my soul,
You hold my heart within your hands,
Together we will make a love that will last forever,

I love you with all that it takes to love,
You will forever be my always,
But you never loved me,
Like I loved you.

I wrote this on 12 September 2017. This poem is another example of thoughts that enter my head. Sometimes I hear something, see something, think of something and I just start writing.

Tell Her

Tell Her,
Don't keep it a secret,
Tell her every day,
Tell her in every way,

Tell her you love her,
And love her with all your soul,

Prove you love,
Prove she can trust you,
And believe in you,

Whisper to her,
Softly each day,
That you love only her,

Steal her kisses,
At every chance you get,
And keep them in your heart,
For times when you're apart,

Take her breath away,
When she least expects it,

Dry her tears,
On the days she cries,
Let her know you are there,

Listen,
With your eyes, ears, and heart,
She will know,
She is most important to you

When it's time,
She gets all your time,
And make her time every day,

Make her laugh,
Tickle her heart and soul,
Make her wear that smile,
That smile that's just for you,

Be proud,
Proud of her, all she does,
To have her by your side,
Proud to show everyone,
She belongs to you,

There is no need for hesitation,
No need to be afraid,
When your heart is true,
Tell her

I finished this poem on 25 February 2013. The inspiration for this poem is simple, how you should love your Lady. Tell her! Don't hold back your emotions. Read the poem again, follow the prompts. It's that simple!!!

Lost

I am lost,
Searching for someone to lose myself in,
To find myself in,
To lay their hands upon my heart,
And show me the light that has faded away,

Falling into the abyss of time,
A quiet sense of something lost,
The once familiar elements of life,
Reduced to nothing more,
Than a hostage of demise I cannot control,

All the haunting memories,
Of dreams that have come undone,
Are but shadows upon the mist,
And I am lost among them,
Trapped in the dark with no windows or doors,

I feel as if I've come to a place,
A place I'd never have to come to,
My soul in division from itself,
And I don't know how I got here,

Wandering and confused,
I stop to rest among the shadows,
But there is no path to follow,
And no sign I was ever here,

I search for the words,
To fill the missing pieces,
To return myself,
A reason to believe,

I am lost,
Still searching for the missing piece,
The one I know I cannot have,
For the whole that can never be filled.

I wrote this poem on 16 June 18. The inspiration for this poem came from a trip to the grocery store one day. It seemed I was the only single person there that day, and I just seemed lost. The more I thought about it, the more I knew I was lost. Hopefully one day I will be found.

Surface

An unsighted Life,
A life living only on the surface,
Their soul passes through everything,
And yet it touches nothing,

Why do they care more about how things look,
Then how things are,
Always willing to take the shortcut,
Missing all the wisdom beyond the skin,

Are you afraid to see what really exits on the other side,
What's behind your blinds,
If your eyes and ears are filled with illusions,
You will never witness the miracles bestowed upon you,

A beautiful heart,
Their light shines through their eyes,
A beautiful heart is not in the outward expression of the body,
But in the heart of the beholder,

Only those with truth inside,
Will recognize truth inside another,
If you only recognize that which is on the surface,
You will never get to the truth within,

Beyond the surface,
You can find treasure, in places you didn't want to search,
You can hear wisdom, in places you have never listened,
You can realize beauty, in places you fail to see,
But only if you start the journey, you didn't want to take,

Look beyond the surface,
See someone for their heart, and only their heart,
Love someone for the beauty found in their heart,
And that heart will always be beautiful to you.

This poem was written on 24 October 2017. This poem is about being superficial, especially when it comes to a person's looks. This is a simple one, if you only judge a person by what you see on the surface, you will miss so much beauty of their heart.

Bodies (**Warning** Adult Themed Poem)

Our passion ignites with just a whisper,
As our bodies burn from sweet anticipation,
A desire uncontrolled,
My senses surge in your essence,

The yearning of our flesh,
Feeling our passion turn into fire,
A fire of the heart,
A veil of yearning consumes us both,

My hands discover your treasures,
My downward journey to taste your heat,
Drowning deeper into you,
The taste of your love so sweet,

The sensation of your fire
Captures my every sense,
As I gently take my key,
And open your tender love,

As we become one,
Time stands still,
Our bodies move as one to the sounds of passion,
We exist only in ecstasy,

We are one breath,
One flesh,
One heart,
One soul,

The peaks of sensual bliss,
Higher and higher we climb together,
So full of energy and fire,
We tremble in boundless pleasure,

Our bodies glisten in passion,
As we collapse together in exhausted breath,
Still hot and burning,

A glowing ember of intimacy.

I wrote this poem on 25 April 2015. The inspiration for this poem came from talking with an old friend. She always likes my poems but challenged me to write something a little sexier. So here ya go.

Everywhere

I was in a hurry to go everywhere,
But I was going nowhere,
I was blind to life in life,
Until I saw the beauty of her heart,

She is the light I've searched for,
The peace I've longed to find,
The answer to my every question,
And the home my heart has imagined,

She is a dreamer,
A philosopher,
She sees the possibilities in me,
That I never could,

Everywhere I go,
I take part of her with me,
I can feel her vibration,
My soul hungers for her in my dreams,
As she becomes a part of everything I do,

Everyday,
Her love fills my life,
Every color comes alive,
And the birds sing ever so sweet,

She lives within my heart,
In everything I touch,
The air I breath,
And every poem I've yet to write,

Just as the light cannot separate from the sun,
Nor the waves from the sea,
I cannot live without her,
For everywhere I go,
She is everything to me.

I wrote this poem on 16 June 2018. Just some more thoughts that ran through my head one day.

The Quiet Heart

The Quiet Heart,
An ocean of addicting silence,
Continually at war,
With completeness and emptiness,

The Quiet Heart,
Time is wasted on time,
With only shadows for company,
Waiting on something, Nothing,

The voice of a Quiet Heart,
Silent as the wind,
Cries of hope that are never answered,
Making no sound as it breaks,

The Quiet Heart with so much to give,
And nothing to give too,
So much life to share,
With so much left unknown,

A Quiet Heart,
Fighting for breath,
Fighting to hold on,
Only to find nothing to hold on too,

A Quiet Heart tries to mend,
Scars of an unwritten future,
Only to remember,
That which you wanted to forget,

The Quiet Heart,
The only place that feels like home,
Watching the whole world fall apart,
And all you can do is stare

I wrote this poem on 12 February 2018. Just some more thoughts that ran through my head one day.

Unconditional Love

Unconditional Love,
Loving someone in their essence,
Loving someone as they are,
No matter what they do, or fail to do,

Unconditional love is a choice,
It is learned and practiced,
A decision made to love regardless of conditions or disappointments,
Loving someone when they are at times unlovable,

Unconditional love is not blind,
Your eyes must be wide open,
You see all the conditions of love,
You see the resolution that nothing is more important than love,

Unconditional love starts with you,
As you know you better than anyone else,
For if you cannot love your perfect imperfections,
You cannot offer the same to others,

Loving unconditionally isn't something you do,
It's something you are,
The drive to give to the wellbeing of another,
And can never be altered by time or distance,

To believe in unconditional love,
Requires a great deal of faith,
To love without need or expectation,
It flows in the face of anger, blame and indifference,

Love is acceptance,
Love is understanding,
Love is appreciation,
And true love is unconditional

I finished this poem on 1 October 2017. This inspiration for this poem is simply how I believe love should be. Love isn't about what someone has, or what they do for a living. Simply for who they are, including all their perfect imperfections. Loving unconditional is to love without expectations. Loving someone no matter the conditions or disappointments. Loving unconditional starts with you. If you cannot love yourself and your flaws, you cannot offer the same to someone else.

Broken Love

I was never prepared for the ending,
I never dreamed of being wounded so deeply,
Until the day our home,
Became a house of broken love,

There was an emptiness growing in her eyes,
Something I'd never seen before,
And though I was all alone in the darkness,
There were signs I should have seen coming,

When she was there,
For me she was gone,
And when I was there,
I was invisible,

When she was down,
I picked her up,
When I fell,
She let go,

Broken vows,
Like looking into a broken mirror,
Knowing it will always be broken,
Always reflecting fractured images of what was,

A tortured mind,
My heart will always remember,
The person who gave me the best memories,
Has become a lifelong nightmare,

I tried holding on,
To her feelings that were already gone,
But her words and actions confirmed,
To her I was already dead,

I'd been living with an evil,
Looking into the eyes of suspicious lies,
A place where pain and sorrow dwell,
In a house of broken love.

This poem was written on 25 November 2017. This poem is personal and difficult one to talk about, and if I explained too much, it would only lead to heartache. I will let this one go with the following advice, if you are in a relationship and your home has become a house of broken love, open your eyes and see the truth. You don't want a life of helplessness and hopelessness. That pain can never be healed, no matter what you do to try and fix it.

Entwined

Lost in each other's silence,
No words are needed,
As we escape the night,
I am blinded to all around me,

Our bodies glisten by candle light,
As I gently draw you near,
A soft kiss upon your lips,
As I tenderly touch your face,

I am captured by your passion,
Breathing softly on my skin,
As I cradle your head gently on my chest,
Nothing can be more beautiful,

Entwined we are,
Body to body,
Braded together,
Heart to heart,

I hunger for your touch,
To be immersed in your warmth,
An eternal bliss,
My soul at perfect rest,

I yearn to hold you longer and longer,
Till the sun's rays announce the day,
Your warmth I crave to feel,
Your touch my air to breath,

And when the night comes,
And my dreams take me away,
It's you I see,
your body next to me I feel,
Entwined in a perfect moment,
and I pray it will not end.

I wrote this poem on 27 Jan 15. Just some more thoughts that ran through my head one day.

The One That Got Away

I often sit and wonder,
Wonder about her,
The One that found me in the darkness,
The One I let get away,

There is a space in my heart,
That no other could ever fill,
Every breath I take,
I still think of her,

Every place I go,
And all the places we didn't,
Has a memory of her,
Because I loved how she loved just being with me,

What becomes of the One we once loved,
The One we will never see again,
My shattered dreams are caught in eternity,
As her soul once walked through mine,

I wish I had chased after her,
Followed her all the way,
Far away from the haze I clung to so hard,
But I could not see the road lead to her,

I didn't take the chance and beg her to stay,
Instead I let her walk away,
She moved on with her life,
And with it my heart,

I'll never forget her smile,
Her presence in my life,
Forever I remember,
The One that got away.

This poem was written on 11 August 2015. This poem is about a woman I loved long ago. She was the one that got away. The one I let get away. It's still painful to think about it, because I loved her so much. One of the most painful things about living with PTSD, is not knowing when you are being detached and drift away. In my mind, everything was good, but to her I was gone. If I only knew then, what I know now, I wouldn't have let her get away.

Her Song

I heard her song on the radio,
A life so long ago,
And in an instant,
I am reliving a distant memory,

Her long blonde hair,
And soft brown eyes,
Body kissed by the sun,
A real-life California Queen,

We were two hearts falling in love,
Everything felt so right,
I cannot forget,
The way she made me feel,

Summer nights in the moonlight,
The sound of the ocean rolling in,
Her song on the radio,
Singing softly in my arms,

Oh, those were some great times,
Those nights we used to sing along,
Living life without a care,
Living a California dream,

I hear her song on the radio,
And I turn it up loud,
Singing of a forgotten love,
Over and Over.

I finished this poem on 30 September 2014. The inspiration for this poem came from my days when I was a younger man and dating a dream. She was intelligent, beautiful, energetic and she kept me grounded. We shared different taste of music, but I listened to what she wanted, as I tried to be a good boyfriend. Unfortunately, I wasn't smart enough to hold on to her, and we went our separate ways in life. And yes, it was all my fault!! I am sure there's a poem in me somewhere about that. Although we haven't spoken since we parted, I remember her fondly. Did I mention she was Blonde, Tan, and amazing! Anyway, I was driving home one day, and her song came on the radio. I was instantly transported back in time. So many memories came rushing back. So I turned up the radio and sang as loud as I could. It really made me miss her and wished I could tell her I was sorry. I wrote this in her honor that day, with the hopes I can one day tell her it is for her. Lesson learned, don't be a jerk guys. Love her unconditionally and show her respect and understanding. If she has a song, turn it up load and sing it to her.

Someone

I look out my window,
Praying to see the light,
So that I don't have to be alone anymore,
I feel so out of place,

I shout in the darkness,
All that shines in me,
I am losing my faith,
Oh where can you be,

I don't know where to look,
I 've looked everywhere,
I fight to embrace the cold,
As the fire slowly dies inside,

I dream day and night,
Like walking in a haze,
Looking for something more,
Then this empty soul,

Is there someone else in the great unknown,
Is there something,
A force beyond my view,
Guiding this lonely heart,

Is there someone who will hear my every word,
Someone who will reach for me,
Wipe away my tears,
And make me their first choice,

If you're out there listening,
And you hear me calling,
Give me a sign,
Let me be to you, Someone.

I finished this poem on 24 September 2014. The inspiration for this poem came from seeing so many couples around me and I was alone. I have been told I'm very picky, I prefer to say I have standards. As a single father, you must have high standards, but that doesn't mean you don't get lonely.

A Kiss and All Was Said

A Kiss and All Was Said,
It is the passion in your eyes,
That gives to them their sweetness,
It is the love in your heart,
That touches my soul,

Our souls meet on lover's lips,
As your love whispers unto my heart,
Love is our true destiny,
And we find it in one another,

I crave you in the most innocent form,
I crave to kiss you in the mornings,
I crave to kiss you goodnight,
And I crave the love you give me,
Each and every day,

I love falling in love,
I've fallen in love so many times,
Every moment of every day,
And it's always with you,

Each day my love grows for you,
And I give all of my love,
only to you,
With the whole of my heart,
For the whole of my life,

A kiss and all was said,
My heart beats in blissful love,
For on this day, and every day,
I call you mine.

I wrote this poem on 3 FEB 2015. The inspiration for this poem came from came from a lady I have written about many times. She was such a passionate kisser, and I loved to taste her lips. A kiss and all was said, and I loved to communicate with her.

What Do You Want

What Do You Want,
It's for sure not what you say,
Cause when its right in front of you,
You give it away,

There's no such thing as Prince Charming,
Or a fairytale come true,
But there are real gentlemen,
Who will love only you,

So why do you say,
I want a gentleman,
Who will treat me like a queen,
When its truly not what you mean,

A Gentleman's heart is very special,
Because he gives with it all,
He respects you as a lady,
And will never let you fall,

So what do you really want,
Say truly what you feel,
Because a Gentleman's broken heart,
Takes longer to heal.

I wrote this poem on 16 October 2013. The inspiration for this poem came from a lady I have written about before. I am a firm believer that you should define your expectations in any relationship. I was raised and have lived by the philosophy to be a gentleman. So when we first started seeing each other, she expressed how she was treated in past relationships. She had always wanted to find a gentleman, her gentleman.

She would always compliment me on treating her like a lady. Opening her door, letting her go first, and surprising her with flowers. Treating her like no man had ever treated her before. So you would think this would be perfect right? Nope. So as we continued to see each other, the more distant she became, the less we would see each other.

I went away on a business trip and hoped the short absence would help remind her of what we have. But it wasn't meant to be. I received the ever popular and personal text message that we needed to talk when I got back. Of course, I knew what this meant, as it has happened many times before. So I responded, "if you are going to say goodbye, you should just say it now", "goodbye in person would be even more painful". Then I got the message "you are an amazing man" you are such a gentleman and treat me like no man has ever treated me", "But I want something else". I didn't have to ask what it was, because I know she went back to the old boyfriend, the A-hole.

So I will leave it at this. Tell your partner what you want. Define your expectations. Don't play with someone's heart, because a gentleman gives all of his to you. And if you break a gentleman's heart, it takes longer to heal.

In The Air Tonight

I should have seen it coming,
I should expect nothing less,
I can feel it coming,
I can feel it in the air tonight,

I don't like waiting for it,
Those moments that interrupt all life,
I can see your face,
The sinful beam you must be wearing,

You forget I was there from the beginning,
I know what you have done,
Your deceptions mounted a foul,
Your intentions only prove self-gain,

I will always remember,
How could I ever forget,
The first time will never be that last time,
You lent your hand to my end,

The reasons you keep your silence,
For me you cannot fool,
It's part of your plot of pain,
To which I am not a visitor,

As you voice to all,
That I am to fault,
Dragging my name through the permissible inferno,
With no regard to who it may hurt,

I can feel it coming,
It's in the air tonight,
And I am tired of waiting,
For you this is the final goodbye.

This poem was written on 6 November 2014. This is about someone whom I really cared for, but she turned out to be two faced and on her own agenda. She would smile in your face, then stab you in the back. I never knew someone could be so evil, and yet make you think they care about you.

ABOUT THE AUTHOR

Michael Morton is a freelance writer and Poet. He has work forthcoming in Leadership, Poetry about PTSD, Inspirational Poetry and Life Lessons for Little People, children's stories that promote values and morals . He is retired from the U.S. Army and served numerous combat tours in Iraq and Afghanistan. He is a recipient of the Purple Heart, Bronze Star Medal for Valor, and Army Commendation Medal for Valor.

www.ingramcontent.com/pod-product-compliance
Lightning Source LLC
Chambersburg PA
CBHW072044040426
42447CB00012BB/3008